THE CHANGING FACE OF
ARGENTINA

Text by DAISY and LES FEARNS
Photography by BOB SMITH

HODDER
Wayland

an imprint of Hodder Children's Books

Produced for Hodder Wayland by
White-Thomson Publishing Ltd
2/3 St Andrew's Place
Lewes BN7 1UP

Editor: Alison Cooper
Designer: Christopher Halls at Mind's Eye Design, Lewes
Proofreader: Philippa Smith
Additional picture research: Shelley Noronha, Glass Onion Pictures

First published in Great Britain in 2003 by Hodder Wayland, an imprint of
Hodder Children's Books.

British Library Cataloguing in Publication Data
Fearns, Les
  The Changing Face of Argentina
   1. Argentina - History - 1983 - Juvenile literature
   I. Title II. Fearns, Daisy III. Argentina

ISBN 0 7502 3990 5

Printed in Hong Kong

Hodder Children's Books
A division of Hodder Headline Limited
338 Euston Road, London NW1 3BH

The website addresses (URLs) included in this book were valid at the time of
going to press. However, because of the nature of the Internet, it is possible
that some addresses may have changed, or sites may have changed or closed
down since publication. While the author, the packager and Publisher regret
any inconvenience this may cause readers, no responsibility for any such
changes can be accepted by either the author, the packager or the Publisher.

Acknowledgements
The publishers would like to thank
the following for their contributions
to this book: Rob Bowden – statistics
research; Peter Bull – map
illustration; Nick Hawken – statistics
panel illustrations. All photographs
are by Bob Smith except: Ricardo
Fermín Chávez pages 8, 31, 39; Anne
L. Smith page 22; South American
Pictures 9, 40, 41.

Contents

1 All Change for Argentina 4

2 Past Times 6

3 Landscape and Climate.......................8

4 Natural Resources 12

5 The Changing Environment...............16

6 The Changing Population...................20

7 Changes at Home 24

8 Changes at Work 36

9 The Way Ahead 44

   Glossary 46

   Further Information 47

   Index 48

All Change for Argentina

Borges station is a small railway station in a northern suburb of Buenos Aires, the capital of Argentina. The station is old – it was built by British engineers over 130 years ago and it looks as if it should be in the south of England, not in South America. But although it is old, it looks new. In the platform café people sit drinking coffee while they wait for their modern, air-conditioned train to arrive.

◀ *Borges station in the Buenos Aires suburb of Olivos.*

▼ *Rides galore in the Parque de la Costa, the theme park in the delta of the River Plata.*

When the railway line was first built it linked the port of Buenos Aires with the huge farms of the Pampas (grasslands). In the early 1990s the line was completely rebuilt as the 'Tren de la Costa'. It no longer links with the Pampas. Buenos Aires has grown too much for that. Now there are houses all along the route – suburbs for the workers of the capital. The line does not even end at the edge of the Pampas. Instead, the 'Tren' takes its passengers to a theme park built in the delta of the River Plata. Roller-coasters and other thrilling rides, and futuristic shows with spectacular special effects, take young Argentinians far away from the old Argentina of the cattle-herding gaucho, the Argentinian cowboy, and well into the twenty-first century.

This is Argentina today, a country which has changed a great deal – a country which is still changing rapidly.

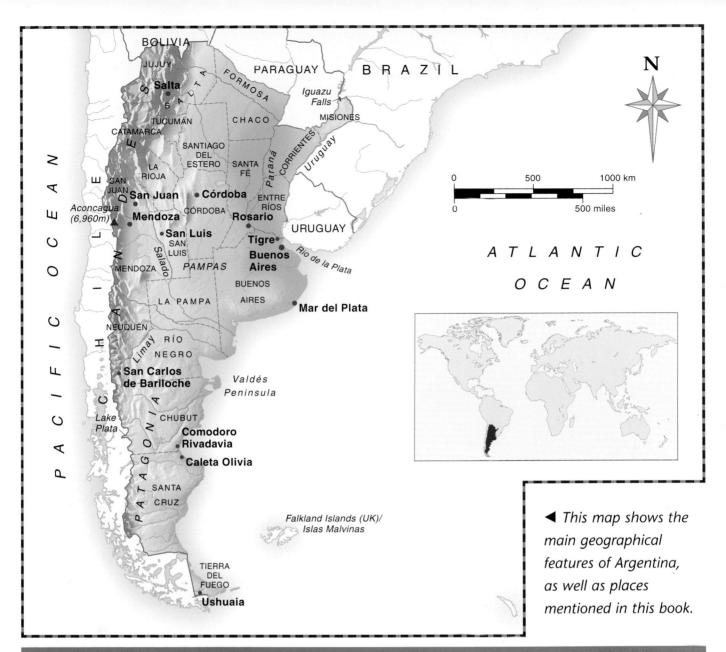

Map labels:

BOLIVIA
PARAGUAY
B R A Z I L
JUJUY
Salta
FORMOSA
Iguazu Falls
TUCUMÁN
CHACO
MISIONES
CATAMARCA
SANTIAGO DEL ESTERO
CORRIENTES
Paraná
Uruguay
LA RIOJA
SANTA FÉ
SAN JUAN
San Juan
Córdoba
ENTRE RÍOS
Aconcagua (6,960m)
Mendoza
CÓRDOBA
Rosario
URUGUAY
San Luis
SAN LUIS
Tigre
Salado
MENDOZA
PAMPAS
Buenos Aires
Río de la Plata
BUENOS AIRES
LA PAMPA
Mar del Plata
NEUQUÉN
Limay
RÍO NEGRO
San Carlos de Bariloche
Valdés Peninsula
Lake Plata
CHUBUT
Comodoro Rivadavia
Caleta Olivia
SANTA CRUZ
Falkland Islands (UK)/ Islas Malvinas
TIERRA DEL FUEGO
Ushuaia

P A C I F I C   O C E A N
A N D E S
P A T A G O N I A

N

0   500   1000 km
0   500 miles

A T L A N T I C   O C E A N

◄ *This map shows the main geographical features of Argentina, as well as places mentioned in this book.*

ARGENTINA: KEY FACTS

Area: 2,766,900 square km

Population: 37,384,816 (2001 est.)

Population density: 13.5 people per square km

Capital city: Buenos Aires (17 million, including Buenos Aires province)

Other main cities: Córdoba (3 million), Rosario (2.9 million), Mendoza (1.6 million)

Highest mountain: Aconcagua (6,960 m)

Longest river: Paraná (4,500 km)

Main language: Spanish

Indigenous languages: Mapuche, Quechua, Guarani, Toba

Major religions: Roman Catholic 92% (although fewer than 20% are active worshippers), Protestant 2%, Jewish 2%, other 4%

Currency: Peso (100 centavos = 1 peso)

2 Past Times

The twentieth century brought difficult times to Argentina. In the late 1920s and 1930s many countries across the world were hit by an economic depression. Trade between countries fell dramatically and many people lost their jobs. Argentina suffered badly and the hardships people were facing led to discontent with the government.

The economic depression led to the first military coups and then, from 1946, to government by Juan Perón. To avoid returning to the problems of the 1930s Perón attempted to make Argentina as independent of the world economy as possible. The country would try to make as many of the goods it needed as it could and not rely on other countries. This proved impossible and Perón was overthrown in 1955.

In 1976 a group of military leaders – a junta – took over and ruled as dictators. Many of their opponents 'disappeared' after being arrested and were never heard of again.

▲ *Juan Perón, leader of Argentina from 1946 to 1955 (centre), and his wife Eva (left), who was known as 'Evita'.*

In 1982 General Galtieri, the leader of the military junta, ordered an invasion of the Falkland Islands. These islands in the South Atlantic were British colonies but Argentina, which calls them the Islas Malvinas, had long claimed them as part of Argentina. Britain recaptured the islands and a combination of the humiliating defeat and economic problems brought down the military junta. A democratic government was set up in Argentina but serious economic problems continued. Hyperinflation made savings worthless and normal day-to-day business became almost impossible.

▲ *The 'Mothers of the Disappeared' demonstrate every Thursday. They are appealing for justice for their missing children, who disappeared during the rule of the military junta.*

In 1988 Carlos Menem was elected president. His economic policies brought stability and prosperity to Argentina for ten years but the boom came to an end in 1998. By 2002 the economy had collapsed. (You can find out more about these events on pages 36–39.) Angry Argentinians took to the streets in protest at the lack of success in solving the country's problems.

IN THEIR OWN WORDS

'I'm Umberto Panos. I used to work in a factory repairing trains in Córdoba. Then, a few years ago, the railways were sold by the government. Most people preferred to travel by coach. It was cheaper and quicker. The railway and the repair factory closed. I lost my job.

'At my age now it is hard to find work. There are other factories but they are closing or do not need so many workers. My daughter lives in Buenos Aires and I came here to stay with her and make some money cleaning shoes. Business people still want their shoes polished and I have my regulars who I enjoy talking to about football.'

3

Landscape and Climate

Argentina is the eighth-largest country in the world and the second-largest country in South America. Uruguay, Paraguay and Brazil lie to the east and north, with Bolivia and Chile to the west. Argentina has a very varied landscape, with high mountains, extensive flat plains, glaciers, deserts, grasslands and rainforest.

The lowland north

Much of this area, north of Córdoba, is tropical or sub-tropical grassland called savannah. This is mixed with forests of thorn trees in the north-west and with rainforest in the far north-east, around the spectacular Iguazu Falls in Misiones. Two major rivers, the Paraná and the Uruguay, form Argentina's north-eastern and eastern borders. They are important resources for hydroelectric power and transport.

The sub-tropical region in the north-west has a hot, dry season between April and September with temperatures of 25–35 °C. This is followed by a rainy season that lasts from October to March, when there is over 100 mm of rain per month. The subtropical region in the north-east has over 75 mm of rain each month and temperatures ranging between 15 and 39 °C throughout the year.

▼ *The Iguazu Falls in north-eastern Argentina.*

IN THEIR OWN WORDS

'*Hola!* My name is Pedro Garcia and I'm 22 years old. I work on an *estancia* (large farm) near San Luis. I have always lived in this area and really enjoy the wide-open space of the Pampas. Mostly I work outside, dealing with the polo ponies we breed. Many of them are exported to other countries. At other times, I help out with the soya bean and sunflower crops. One day I'd like to have the chance to breed my own polo ponies.'

The Pampas

This enormous flat plain of about 1.5 million square kilometres is made up of fine wind-blown soils called loess. Here the summers (November to January) are hot and dry, with temperatures of 25–35 °C. Winters (June to August) are mild, with temperatures of 5–10 °C.

There are few rivers in this region, and when heavy rains do occur they can cause flooding. This is because the land slopes only gently towards the Atlantic Ocean and the rainfall takes time to flow away. Hardly any trees grow here naturally, but eucalyptus have been planted by landowners to shelter their animals and crops from the wind and sun. The Pampas is Argentina's major agricultural area, where raising cattle and growing wheat are both important activities.

▼ *Gauchos at work on the Pampas. Windmills, used to pump water, are a common sight in this region.*

The Andes

This rugged mountain range has an average height of over 3,000 metres and contains many volcanoes, deep valleys and the highest peak in South America – Aconcagua at 6,960 metres. Earthquakes are common in this region.

Patagonia and the far south

To the east of the Andes in southern Argentina lies a desert-like stony plateau that gently slopes down to the South Atlantic Ocean. Here in Patagonia very little rain falls – just 130 mm per year. The strong, warm Zonda wind blows down from the mountains, keeping the temperature between 5 °C and 25 °C.

The world's most southerly city of Ushuaia is on the island of Tierra del Fuego. In the far south of Argentina the winter is very cold and dark, and it is not very warm even during the short summer, with average temperatures of 12 °C. Argentina also considers part of the Antarctic continent as its territory, where polar conditions occur.

▲ *The Andes mountain chain runs for nearly 3,500 km along the western border with Chile.*

Climate change

Increased rainfall, a rise in sea-level and higher temperatures have all been recorded in Argentina as an indication of gradual climate change. In 1997–98 increased rainfall and flooding in Argentina was linked to El Niño, a change in the flow of air and sea currents in the Pacific Ocean that occurs every few years. There is some evidence that El Niño events are becoming more frequent and the effects on the world's climate more severe.

▲ The Rio Salado in full flood in San Luis province.

If global warming were to cause a rise in the sea-level of around one metre, it would flood areas such as Buenos Aires and other coastal developments. Long-term changes in the climate would also affect agriculture – for example, by making it too hot, dry or wet for some crops to grow.

IN THEIR OWN WORDS

'My name is Willy Bryant and I'm a warden in the Wildlife Sanctuary in San Isidro. Many different species of bird and animal make their homes in this protected area and all sorts of migrating birds make stops here on their long journeys too.

'Over 1,250 schoolchildren visited the sanctuary last year for guided tours. They learn about the wildlife and the big pollution problems we have to deal with, which are caused by flooding. We are getting flooded by the river more and more often, but luckily there are many volunteers to help clean up.

'It's important that areas like this are carefully managed for the future. I'm pleased that nature reserves and national parks are becoming more popular with tourists and local people every year.'

4

Natural Resources

Minerals

Argentina gets its name from the Latin word for silver – *argentum*. Until the early nineteenth century, silver was the single biggest export from Argentina, making up 80 per cent of all exports. Today silver is only mined on a small scale because the deposits are too small for large-scale mining to be worthwhile. There are also deposits of lead, zinc, iron ore, copper, tin, gold and uranium, but mining these minerals is not a major industry.

Energy sources

Today most of the electricity Argentina needs is produced by coal-fired power stations or by hydroelectric power plants, using dams on rivers such as the Limay, Paraná and Uruguay. Nuclear power supplies over 12 per cent of the country's electricity needs. There are plans to use wind-generated power as an alternative energy source. However, economic difficulties mean that Argentina is unlikely to be able to develop new power sources in the near future.

The oil and gas industry has become more developed since the mid 1980s and it began exporting oil in 1996. There are onshore oil fields around Comodoro Rivadavia and Caleta Olivia in southern Argentina and additional fields are now being exploited around Salta, in the north-west. Undersea oil and natural gas deposits are being explored near the Islas Malvinas (Falkland Islands) under a joint agreement between Argentina and Britain.

▲ *Silver is used to make traditional gaucho ornaments, picture frames and jewellery, which are sometimes sold as tourist souvenirs.*

Forestry

Natural forests of both hardwood, such as oak and cedar, and softwood, such as pine, still exist and are found mainly in mountain areas. There are also big new plantations where softwoods like Paraná pine, elm, willow and eucalyptus are grown. The timber from these trees is used to make paper and chipboard. Wood is still used extensively as a fuel for cooking too, either as logs or charcoal. Red *quebracho* wood is used in the leather-tanning process.

▲ *Yacimientos Petroliferos Fiscales (YPF) is the largest national oil company. Products from its refinery and processing plant near Mendoza are exported to Chile, Uruguay, Brazil and Paraguay.*

IN THEIR OWN WORDS

'*Hola!* My name is Hugo Ibañe and I've been a taxi driver in Buenos Aires for seven years. I enjoy meeting lots of different people – in my job you never know who is going to get in the back! The city is very busy, noisy and quite polluted. Two years ago the company I work for changed all the taxis so that they only use Liquid Petroleum Gas (LPG). It doesn't have to be imported, it's cheaper to produce than petrol and causes a bit less pollution.'

Agriculture

Agriculture is Argentina's main natural resource. Nine per cent of all land is used for growing crops and over 48 per cent is pasture for beef and dairy cattle. Farms called *estancias* cover huge areas – 4,000 hectares is considered a small farm. In the past *estancias* were all family owned, but today some are run by co-operatives.

Wheat has traditionally been an important crop and is still produced on a very large scale. Soya, sorghum, sunflowers and maize, which are processed to produce oils for the food industry, are grown in increasing quantities. Production of soya, for example, jumped from just under 4 million tonnes in 1980 to almost 19 million tonnes in 2000.

Argentina exports large amounts of raw and processed meats, live animals and leather all over the world. Sheep are kept for their wool, but production has fallen since the 1980s, from 157,000 tonnes in 1980 to 122,000 tonnes in 2000. This is because demand for wool has declined, due to the increased use of artifical fibres in the textile industries.

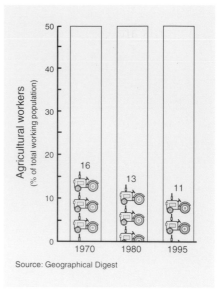

Source: Geographical Digest

▲ *The number of agricultural workers has fallen steadily since 1970, as a result of more efficient methods of farming.*

◄ *Beef cattle are herded by* estancia *workers – gauchos – before being taken to market. Over 2,500 head of cattle are reared on this* estancia *in San Luis province.*

Wine

Vineyards are found in the foothills of the Andes Mountains around Mendoza and San Juan. New processing methods introduced since the mid 1990s have greatly expanded wine production. Although Argentinians are drinking less wine, exports of fine wines have increased by 900 per cent. Argentina is now amongst the five largest wine producers in the world.

Fishing

The main fishing port is Mar del Plata, 400 km south of Buenos Aires. The fishing industry has declined because Argentinians prefer to eat more beef than fish, especially as beef is often cheaper to buy. Over 90 per cent of the catch is exported to other South American countries, but export markets do not make up for reduced sales in Argentina.

▲ *Vines being grown in a vineyard near Mendoza. The grapes will be used to produce fine Malbec wines, which will be exported to Europe, the USA, Canada and South Africa.*

IN THEIR OWN WORDS

'*Buenos dias!* I'm Tono Pernas and my family has owned this *estancia* for 80 years. We enjoy living close to nature out on the Pampas. The way we farm has changed a lot in my lifetime, thanks to new technology. Mechanical planting and harvesting, for example, is a big improvement on doing it all by hand! We now use GM seeds, too, as they produce better crops.

'In the future we hope to extend our cattle grazing and also to grow peanuts. One day the family may decide to sell the land and just manage the business for a big co-operative.'

The Changing Environment

Air pollution

In Buenos Aires air pollution caused by the vehicles that clog the city's roads is a serious problem. Every day the newspapers publish the levels of air pollution for Buenos Aires, as a warning to people who have chest problems, such as asthma, to take extra care. Industries produce 43 per cent of air pollution, transportation produces 33 per cent and the remaining 24 per cent comes from homes and businesses. The Kyoto Protocol – an international agreement in 1997 to reduce greenhouse gases – may help to improve the situation in the future. Argentina has volunteered to reduce carbon emissions by 2010.

Water pollution

Industrial, agricultural and domestic waste continues to be dumped in landfill sites near water supplies or directly into rivers, causing serious pollution. Although there are laws

◄ The ferryman rows paying passengers across the polluted waterway called Riachuelo, in La Boca, a district of Buenos Aires. Raw sewage as well as rubbish can be seen and smelled every day.

against dumping waste in this way, they are often ignored. Since the late 1990s Aguas Argentinas, the national water board, has been improving the ageing sewage systems and the quality of the water supply to people's homes in Buenos Aires. However, many people still drink only bottled water.

Recycling

Recycling is mainly carried out by individuals, who collect, sort and then sell or re-use material that has been thrown away. In 1999 small collection bins for recycling glass and tins were introduced, but not everyone uses them. Some paper recycling is organized by companies that produce paper products.

▶ *Ricardo, Ignacio and Sergio are brothers who spend their afternoons collecting drink cans from the city streets. They sell them to help buy food for the family.*

IN THEIR OWN WORDS

'My name is Adriana Vodovosoff and I'm a teacher. In school, the children learn the '3 Rs' of global pollution issues – Recycle, Reduce and Re-use. Four years ago we started our Eco Campaign and set targets each term. When we've collected 1,000 kg of newspapers they are sent for recycling into paper tissues and table napkins. We try hard to reduce the amount of paper we use in school, by using both sides of each sheet before it's recycled.

'In the future I'd like to see more laws to reduce air pollution, to tackle the problem of all the buses, lorries and factories which pump dirty gases into the atmosphere.'

City life

Over 13 million people live in the overcrowded and polluted capital city. Rising crime rates and personal safety are increasing daily worries for many who live in the city. Most office buildings and many apartment blocks have a 24-hour guard. Around private houses there are high metal railings and most have an entry-phone, too. Some *Porteños* (people who live in Buenos Aires) are planning to move out to live in quieter, safer and healthier areas.

Many of the more traditional, colonial-style family homes, with an internal patio or garden, are being knocked down. This is happening to make way for even more high-rise apartment blocks, with little or no outdoor space. A large percentage of *Porteños* live in apartments.

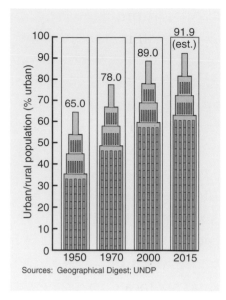

▲ By 2015 it is expected that the great majority of Argentinians will be living in urban areas.

◀ Tall apartment blocks have been built in Belgrano in Buenos Aires to provide more homes for those who want to live in the city.

New communities

For a small minority of families, who have enough money, one way to live in more pleasant and safer surroundings is to move out of the city and live in one of the new 'countrys'. These landscaped communities, protected by gates and fences, provide houses with gardens. The 'countrys' also provide kindergartens and schools, leisure facilities, shops, banks, medical centres and security guards, who are on duty at the access gates. 'Countrys' such as Nordelta and Estancia del Pilar are located around the edges of Buenos Aires. New roads and extensions to existing railway lines are being built to allow commuters to travel easily to work in the city centre.

▶ *A security guard at the entrance to the Nordelta 'country'.*

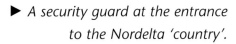

IN THEIR OWN WORDS

'Welcome to our new home! I'm Mariana Brugo and I moved to Nordelta with my family in 2000. We had been living in the city in an apartment, where our growing family was running out of room! We had also been burgled twice, so extra security was a very important reason for moving here.

'Now my family enjoys the space and the peaceful surroundings, and we don't even have to travel far to visit shops or the health centre. The weather is very different from in the city, we get lots of mosquitoes in the summer and fog in the winter months, but we really prefer living here. It's a great place for children to grow up.'

The Changing Population

Who are the Argentinians?

Modern Argentina is a mix of people from different backgrounds. Only a small number (3 per cent) are native South Americans. Today this indigenous population is found mainly in the poorer northern provinces of the Chaco and Jujuy.

The other 97 per cent of Argentinians are descended from European immigrants. The Spanish came first, in the sixteenth century, and settled in the first towns. Soon, they moved out of the towns and into the countryside. Later, they built ranches, or *estancias*, on the vast Pampas. They successfully fought a series of wars against the native South Americans and the numbers of native South Americans soon fell.

A thriving cattle industry grew up and by 1900 Argentina was amongst the ten wealthiest countries in the world. This prosperity attracted more European immigrants. Most were from Italy, but Swiss and Germans also came and settled in the north, where they became successful farmers. Basque, Irish and Welsh communities grew up in the sheep-herding areas of Patagonia.

▲ *La Boca, the district of Buenos Aires where many of the poorest immigrants first settled. It has become a major tourist attraction – and the home of Boca Juniors, the team that the famous footballer Maradona played for.*

IN THEIR OWN WORDS

'I'm Mary Kowalczewski and I'm the daughter of a Polish immigrant. My parents left Poland at the start of the Second World War in 1939 and after living in England for a while we came to Argentina in 1949, when I was 10 years old. Settling in was hard at first but we made many friends who, like us, were also Polish immigrants. This made life in our new country much easier.

'I am married to an Argentinian doctor and I have four grown-up children. Argentina is the homeland for my own children and grandchildren but I still like to have links with Poland. The Internet has made this much easier. I listen to Polish radio on the web, which keeps me in touch and gives me an opportunity to use the Polish language.'

The majority of immigrants stayed in the capital, Buenos Aires. Today the results of this immigrant mix can be seen everywhere – for example, there are Italian restaurants, German language newspapers and Scottish country dancing clubs. Many Argentinians have two passports, an Argentinian passport and a passport from their family's country of origin in Europe.

▶ *Argentina's newspapers are produced in many different languages to meet the needs of its population.*

Argentina's new migrants

In many ways Argentina is more like a European country than a Latin American one. Its figures for life expectancy (75.2 years) and infant mortality (18 deaths per 1,000 live births), for example, follow the pattern of western Europe rather than the pattern of most of its Latin American neighbours.

The statistics give an impression of a prosperous, healthy society but this is only part of the modern story. Indigenous people from the poorer regions of Argentina migrate to the capital to look for work. Indigenous people from the neighbouring countries of Bolivia, Paraguay and Peru also come to Buenos Aires. Many of these migrants are living in extreme poverty.

When they find work it is often low-paid, manual work. Many women work as maids in wealthier people's houses.

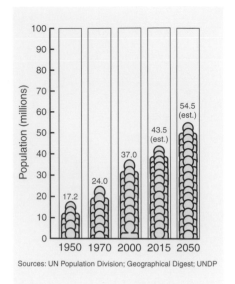

Sources: UN Population Division; Geographical Digest; UNDP

▲ *Argentina's population more than doubled in the second half of the twentieth century and is expected to carry on growing rapidly.*

▼ *An Argentinian family living in the poor northern province of Chaco.*

IN THEIR OWN WORDS

'I'm Esteban Shannon and I work with community groups in local *villas*. In many *villas* people are trying hard to improve basic facilities by providing water and electricity for themselves. Outside groups like the Church help. Elections provide an opportunity for politicians to take an interest in improving *villa* conditions.

'Some people eventually move out of the *villas*. With a good job they can live elsewhere. Sometimes, people who have come here from other countries return home if they cannot get work. However it is hard for children who grow up in the *villas*. They often do not get the education or skills they need to find well-paid work. These are the people who will stay in the *villas*.'

They live in shanty towns in and around Buenos Aires. In Argentina these shanty towns are known as *villas* (pronounced 'vishas'). Living conditions in the *villas* are poor. Few have services like piped clean water, sewerage and electricity supplies. Here infant mortality is higher than the national average, at 52 deaths per 1,000 live births.

Like the Europeans who came earlier, the new migrants hope to find a good job, settle with their families and leave the *villas*. However, this is proving very difficult. It is hard for people to gain the education that will take them into the better-paid jobs of the modern economy.

▲ *Shanty towns, or* villas, *like these can be found throughout Buenos Aires.*

7

Changes at Home

Family life

The traditional idea of the family, with the man earning money for the family and the woman staying at home as wife and mother, is still very important in Argentina. It is quite common for an extended family of parents, grandparents and even married children to share the family home. Renting or buying a home is very expensive so young married couples often live with their parents because they cannot afford a home of their own.

◀ This father and son team collects and recycles goods that the inhabitants of Olivos throw out. Working together as a family is a common feature of life in Argentina, especially among poorer families.

IN THEIR OWN WORDS

'I'm Maria Jose Ferreyra, and I was born in Córdoba, where three generations lived in the same house. I remember the relaxed, carefree atmosphere in which we all lived. That's different from today, as I live with my husband and children in an apartment in the centre of Buenos Aires. City life is hectic and can be unsafe.

'Unlike my mother or grandmother, I have a full-time job. It's hard to find time for housework and to look after the children as well – I have a maid for a few hours each weekday, and my husband shares some of the chores.

'There have been a lot of changes in family life since I was a child, but I probably want the same for my children as my mother wanted for me – I want them to be happy and successful and to make me a grandmother one day!'

Although traditionally it is men who have gone out to work, since the early 1990s more married women have taken jobs outside the home. Attitudes towards working women have become more relaxed and women want to go out to work and earn money. When both parents work, the children are usually looked after by other family members, or by a maid if the family can afford it.

Spending time together as a family is considered very important. Most families have an evening meal together – it's a time to talk and listen to everyone's news, from grandpa to the youngest member of the family. Going out as a family is also a regular activity, whatever the age of the children. The second Sunday in August is Dia del Niños or Children's Day. It's a big celebration with parties and presents – just like having another birthday!

▶ *Clara Astolfi collects her school lunch from Victoria, who is the family's maid. Victoria lives in the Astolfi's home and works for them six days a week.*

Shopping

In every *barrio*, or neighbourhood, there is a selection of shops selling fresh produce: the *panadería* (bakery), *carnecería* (butcher) and *verdulería* (greengrocer). There is also a kiosk that sells sweets, snacks, milk and soft drinks. Each *barrio* will also have at least one supermarket.

Along the main roads of the towns there are other shops and businesses. These are mostly small and family run. They specialize in selling one type of product. A *cotillón*, for example, only sells goods that people need to give a birthday party. The *librería* sells school books and equipment, as all children take everything they need to use in school every day.

A newer type of shop is the bazaar – a shop that sells anything from picture frames to shopping bags or clothes pegs to perfumed candles. The bazaars sell goods imported from China, and they are very popular, as everything is very cheap.

▲ *This* verdulería *always has a wide range of fresh fruit and vegetables. It is usual to buy produce every day.*

In the early 1990s the first large shopping centre was opened in San Isidro, a northern suburb of Buenos Aires. Unicenter has doubled in size since it was first opened and now has multi-screen cinemas, food courts, a supermarket, a department store and over 100 other shops and facilities.

In the USA and many other countries shopping malls have largely replaced smaller, local shops. In Argentina, the *panadería*, *librería*, *carnecería* and *verdulería*, just around the corner from people's homes, continue to do good business.

▶ *Unicenter's main plaza. It's a popular place to stop and have a coffee or helados (freshly made ice-cream). Unicenter is the only development on this scale in the whole of Argentina.*

IN THEIR OWN WORDS

'Hi, my name's Diego Martin Duarte and I'm 20 years old. I've worked in Unicenter for nearly a year. It's great working here; it's very comfortable – cool in the summer and warm in the winter – and so different from working in small neighbourhood shops.

'In the bookshop where I work, I enjoy helping customers, some local and others from all over the world. When I'm not working I'm usually spending money here, in some of the tempting clothes or shoe shops, or watching a movie. Even better, I get a discount!'

Changes in diet
In Argentina traditional foods are still very popular. Lunch or dinner would not be complete without *carne*, a beef dish. This is not surprising, as the cattle *estancias* produce some of the best beef in the world. The meat is usually cooked on a *parrilla* or barbecue.

Snack foods such as *empanadas* – small pastry pies with different fillings – are cheap and delicious, as are *alfajores* – two or three crumbly biscuits sandwiched together with *dulce de leche* (sweet caramel) and covered with chocolate too! In the late afternoon, most people have coffee and *facturas*, which are tasty cakes and pastries.

The afternoon snacks keep people going until the family meal in the evening, which does not usually begin until after 10 pm. Even the children stay up until this time and eat with

▲ *Meat cooked on a* parrilla *has a wonderful flavour. Apartment blocks have communal* parrillas *on the roof and most houses have one in the garden.*

IN THEIR OWN WORDS

'My name is Paula Lanusse and I'm 19 years old. I work as a cook for a family and the workers on an *estancia* in the province of San Luis. Traditionally, men do the cooking on a *parrilla*, so it's quite unusual to find a female cook. I prepare fresh beef twice a day, and nothing is ever left over or wasted. I think there'd be trouble if I tried to change the menu!

'What I'd really like to do in the future is to live in a big city, like Buenos Aires, and work in a restaurant.'

their parents. After eating so late in the evening it is perhaps not surprising that breakfast is only a hot drink and a slice of toast, or is missed out completely.

The influence of immigrants from Europe on Argentinian food can be seen on any menu or supermarket shelf. Pasta and pizza are firm favourites with most families. *Milanesa* and *papas fritas* – thin slices of beef or chicken, coated in breadcrumbs and served with chips, is another popular dish that was introduced by the European settlers; *helados* – fresh, flavoured ice-cream – was also brought to Argentina from Europe.

In the 1990s international fast food chains arrived in the country and they are now popular with younger people. The Unicenter Food Court offers oriental and Mexican cuisine. But there are growing concerns that a change in eating habits is leading to more people becoming seriously overweight. This is because people are eating more processed foods, which have a higher fat content than freshly prepared foods.

▼ *Freshly cooked pizza is just one of the many meals that can be ordered over the telephone and delivered to people's homes.*

Education

Argentina has one of the highest basic literacy rates (96 per cent) in Latin America. All pupils receive nine years of schooling but education is not compulsory after Year 9 (usually aged 15). Many young people leave at this stage and look for work, instead of staying on until the age of 18 and completing their secondary education.

▲ *These pupils from a school near Mendoza are in the uniform of white coats worn across Argentina.*

Education is under much pressure to change. To make it possible for more pupils to gain a secondary education the government has introduced reforms to the curriculum but because of lack of money there are not enough teachers or books in many state schools. As a result, 23 per cent of teenagers still do not complete a secondary education. Public education is free, but private education at school and university level is expanding for those who can afford it. There are 86 universities, 49 of which are private.

University education is well respected and of a high standard. The University of Buenos Aires has 200,000 students, but as many as 60 per cent of undergraduates do not finish their studies. Often, this is because students have to do paid work at the same time as studying and it becomes too difficult to do both. Many of those who do finish cannot find suitable work in Argentina. In recent years more and more have been leaving to work in Europe or the USA.

Healthcare and the welfare system

Ever since the time of Perón (see pages 6–7) Argentina has provided basic health and welfare provision for all. A national insurance scheme ensures that even the poorest can be treated in clinics and hospitals, and provides pensions. Argentinian women receive maternity benefits such

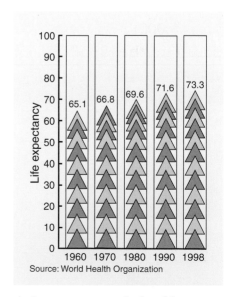

Source: World Health Organization

▲ *Improvements in health care have contributed to the increase in life expectancy.*

IN THEIR OWN WORDS

'I am Doctor Raul DeMarco and I am happy to say there have been many improvements in healthcare in Argentina. Public hospitals treat people who do not have or cannot pay for private medical insurance. Private hospitals are for those who can afford to pay.

'However the universities train large numbers of doctors and the country can no longer afford to employ them all.'

as a full salary for 90 days of their maternity leave, cash grants before and after birth and monthly family allowances for each child.

Many improvements have been made to the health and welfare system but serious problems with the economy since the end of the 1990s have made it very difficult for the government to meet the costs. For people without private insurance, medical care is now getting worse and they may have to rely on a local charity hospital for treatment. It is also more difficult to obtain imports of vital medicines, and the government is struggling to pay pensions. Good health also depends on where you live. Twice as many (84 out of every 1,000) Argentinians die of infectious disease in the poorer north than in Buenos Aires, because of poor sanitation and a lack of medical facilities outside the cities.

◀ *A local chemist, or* farmacia. *It has become much harder to buy medicines as Argentina's economic problems have worsened.*

Leisure

Football has long been a national passion. People not only love to support the famous teams like Boca Juniors or River Plate, they also enjoy playing football in any open space, or watching it on one of the TV sport channels.

For the minority of families that can afford them, sporting clubs offer a range of activities that are available throughout the year. Every *barrio* or neighbourhood has well-used squares and parks. They all contain shaded areas with benches and play areas that are busy with families, all day and well into the night. At weekends and during holidays some squares have craft stalls and live entertainment.

▶ *Local parks are busy places on Sundays. Children and adults play football all day.*

IN THEIR OWN WORDS

'I'm Fernando Mansilla, I'm 33 and I'm a graphic designer. I've played football ever since I could crawl. My friends and I play five-a-side, after work and at the weekends. I'm a big Boca Juniors fan and go to watch them play – if I can get a ticket. Boca Juniors have produced many world-class players, like Maradona and Verón, and their stories are celebrated in a unique museum.

'I also watch every Liverpool match on cable TV. I support Liverpool, not only to watch good football, but because it's the place where my favourite music comes from – The Beatles!'

Going to the cinema is a regular leisure activity, especially on Wednesdays, when tickets are half price. Tango, the music and dance, started in the poorest dock areas in the early 1900s and was popular until the 1940s. Recently, tango has become fashionable again, with classes available for all age groups.

Entertainment in the capital is like that in many European cities. It ranges from pop music concerts and clubs, to plays, ballet, classical music and opera. There is also much street theatre and many exhibitions.

Videos, computer games and DVDs are now widely available for hire, as buying them is very expensive. Since the mid 1990s the number of Internet service providers has greatly increased, as more and more people want to use the Internet, either from their own homes or from the growing number of Internet cafés.

◀ *These tango dancers are performing in a street in the San Telmo district of Buenos Aires.*

Communications

Since the early 1990s there has been a big improvement in communications in Argentina. In the 1980s it was very difficult to get a telephone connection to your house. Occasionally, the apartments in a block shared one telephone line. Families sometimes moved from one house to another because there was a working telephone line. Public phones were few and far between, located on noisy street corners – and did not always work.

Today, there are more than 8 million private telephone lines, compared with just over 1 million in 1980, and most homes have at least one telephone. Both public and private telephone lines have become much more reliable. For people who do not have their own telephone, there are many new *locutorios* or telephone centres, where calls can be made or the Internet used to read or send e-mail.

In 1991 cellular (mobile) telephones were introduced and the number of people using mobiles continues to increase every year. The cellular network does not yet cover the whole of Argentina.

▼ *This* locutorio *is regularly used by local residents, to make long-distance telephone calls or to 'surf the net'.*

In the cities using the Internet is cheap and the level of use is higher than in western Europe. Argentina is pioneering high-speed wireless Internet, where web access is by microwave radio transmission, instead of via telephone cables. This will help to bring the web to the 15 million Argentinians who live in remote rural areas, where dial-up connection is very expensive. This includes the Patagonian Andes where telephone lines are scarce or not available.

ConectAr is a joint state–private industry project set up to link schools with a chain of microwave transmitters. There are hopes that schemes like this will be able to make the Internet available cheaply to remote public schools which have few learning resources.

▶ *Remote communities like this one in San Luis province will benefit from improved telecommunications.*

IN THEIR OWN WORDS

'I'm George Garcia Posadas and I'm 74 years young! The telephone service used to be terrible; you had to wait for an operator to connect you to the number and making a long-distance call could take hours. You waited years to have a new phone line installed in your house or office. Today the telephone system is very efficient, but quite expensive. For the past three years I have used a mobile phone; it means I'm always available and easy to contact, for both my business and my family.'

8

Changes at Work

The new economy of the 1990s

In the mid-1980s Argentina, like many other South American countries, was hit by soaring inflation. The price of goods rose very fast – eventually they were doubling every month. People's wages became worthless – they could not afford to buy even basic items.

In 1988 Carlos Menem was elected president. He brought an end to hyperinflation by bringing in a new currency, the peso. The value of the peso was made equal to one US dollar. This policy was called dollar convertibility.

At the same time the government sold many of the state businesses such as railways, airlines, gas, electricity, water and postal services and invited foreign companies to invest in Argentina. A trading partnership, modelled on the European Community, was set up with Brazil, Uruguay and Paraguay. It was called Mercosur.

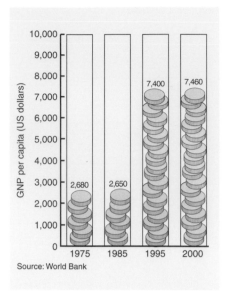

Source: World Bank

▲ In the late 1980s and early 1990s there was very strong growth in the Argentinian economy.

◄ The expansion of Ezeiza airport reflected the growth of international trade during Carlos Menem's presidency.

IN THEIR OWN WORDS

'I'm Juan Carlos and I have worked in the fruit market in Tigre since 1937. Up until 1972, the family grew fruit and nuts and sold them to a wholesaler. Today we sell locally made baskets and handicrafts. We have a boat – *Huaglen* – which we use as a floating stall selling honey, homemade jams and plants. We're here every weekend, as the market is popular with both local people and tourists; we earn more today than we did in the past. The market is changing every year and there are more plans to develop other parts of the old port.'

For ten years these policies brought the prosperity and stability that Argentina desperately needed. European companies rushed to invest in the country, controlling much of the new economy. Along with Mercosur, Europe was Argentina's main trading partner, providing 28 per cent of imports into Argentina and buying 21 per cent of Argentina's exports (worth US$26.5 billion) by 2000.

The economy grew at a rate of around 6 per cent a year, the highest growth rate in Latin America. Many Argentinians had more money to spend than ever before and shops of all kinds did good business. Government money was spent in the poorer provinces to provide work on schemes such as road building and constructing dams. The Argentinian economy was seen as a model for many other developing world economies.

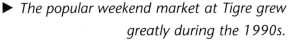

▶ *The popular weekend market at Tigre grew greatly during the 1990s.*

Economic crisis

Although Argentina's economy appeared to be doing very well in the 1990s, there were underlying problems. One of these was the policy of dollar convertibility. This had helped to stabilize the economy in the late 1980s but it meant that Argentina had less control over its economy than its Mercosur neighbours. Other Mercosur countries reduced the value of their currencies in the late 1990s. The price of the goods they were offering for sale abroad became cheaper than goods made in Argentina. Overseas owners began to close down their factories in Argentina.

▲ *As the dollars ran out, local currencies appeared alongside the dollar and the peso.*

As the economy slowed down the government had to cut what it spent on schools, hospitals and welfare. It also borrowed a great deal from overseas banks. Provinces began to print their own money. Soon several currencies were in use:

- the official Argentine peso
- the US dollar
- money such as *patacones*, issued by local provinces to part-pay pensions, benefits and salaries.

It was not only the government that had borrowed money. Shoppers had bought on credit, and companies had expanded with loans from the new (mainly European) banks. When the boom ended these loans could not be repaid. Argentina was forced to rely on loans from the International Monetary Fund.

As the economy collapsed, unemployment rose to 25 per cent. The government could not afford to pay its workers. In the cities 44 per cent of the population were officially classified as poor, with an income of less than 120 pesos a month.

IN THEIR OWN WORDS

'I'm Umberto Galitelli. I work in a bank in the Microcentro – the financial district of Buenos Aires. During the 1990s we did well. My bank became part of a big European group of businesses and was modernized. Many customers had even begun to use the Internet to do their banking. When dollar convertibility ended my job became much harder. The banks were closed for a long time to stop people taking all their money out and customers became very angry. Then their money fell in value as the peso grew weak. This made them even angrier. I think many Argentinians do not trust banks any more. They prefer to keep their savings at home – under the bed or in the garage!'

Finally, in 2002, dollar convertibility was ended and the peso was devalued. People now saw their savings become worthless in relation to the US dollar. Angry demonstrators brought down a succession of governments as politicians struggled to find a way ahead. At the time this book was written politicians were still trying to find a way to deal with the crisis.

▼ Cacerolazos – *demonstrators banging pots and pans in protest – became a familiar sight on the streets of Buenos Aires during the economic crisis of 2001–2002.*

Tourism

One area of the economy that might be boosted by the fall in the value of the peso is tourism. The weakness of the peso has made Argentina a less expensive place for foreign tourists to visit.

Argentina has huge potential as a tourist destination. On offer are the magnificent Iguazu Falls in the north, set in sub-tropical rainforest. By contrast the south has the Moreno Glacier National Park in Patagonia. The Moreno Glacier is one of only a few in the world that are advancing – getting longer as a result of the large amounts of ice that form each winter. In between there is whale watching off the Valdés Peninsula and the world-famous penguin and seal colonies of Chubut. In the west there are the Andes, with one of the world's most active volcanoes, Antofalla. The same mountains also offer skiers one of the main skiing complexes of the southern hemisphere, at Bariloche.

▲ *The beach resort of Mar del Plata is already extremely popular with Argentinian holidaymakers.*

IN THEIR OWN WORDS

'My name is Graciela Sautner and I'm a travel agent in Martinez in Buenos Aires. Over the last eight years, many more overseas visitors have come to Argentina. We now have a Ministry for Tourism, which advertises Argentinian attractions like the Iguazu Falls all over the world. Big European companies are now using Argentina for incentive travel – holidays offered as rewards to company workers who perform well.

'My office deals with both holidays and business travel arrangements. In the past, it often took quite a while to contact hotels and clients, but today I use the Internet to take and make bookings. Looking ahead, I expect to offer a wider range of holidays, like adventure holidays. Trekking, white-water rafting, whale watching, riding and fishing are becoming very popular. The two things that most people want to experience in Argentina are tango and Patagonia – we can still provide both of these!'

The government recognizes that many of the attractions have not been promoted as well as they could have been. Tourism could provide much-needed work in many of the least prosperous areas of the country and bring in valuable foreign currency. The essentials for tourism already exist: the attractions are easily accessible and Argentina has many world-class hotels. The challenge the country faces is to attract enough international tourists.

▶ *Tourists on a whale-watching trip off the Valdés Peninsula in Patagonia.*

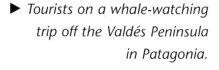

Women at work

Since 1980 the number of women going out to work has increased by a third to over 35 per cent of the workforce. In some ways the work that women do has not changed. It is still very common for even middle-class families to have a maid, and as many as 20 per cent of all working women work as maids. They often live at home with their employers, returning to their own family at the weekend. They do the manual work around the house: cleaning, sweeping, cooking and often doing the food shopping. They earn around $400 a month.

▼ *A female cleaner at Borges station in Buenos Aires.*

▲ *A woman at work on school crossing patrol duty on a busy road in Buenos Aires.*

IN THEIR OWN WORDS

'I'm Alejandra Taormina. As well as running my own business I belong to a group of women entrepreneurs who meet regularly to help promote the success of women in business.

'In the past women managers were not really taken seriously by men. Women were often believed to be not up to the job. Nowadays attitudes are different but women are still not accepted as equals. We are often treated more like competitors who have to be challenged by men in the workplace.

'To succeed, women need to be very focused and well organized. You need to be able to do several different things at the same time. I am optimistic that each year more women will be successful in Argentinian business.'

What has changed is the number of more prosperous and educated women who now work and want to have careers. Teaching has always been popular, as it is respected if not well-paid work. The prosperity of the 1990s led to more opportunities for women in new areas such as media, law, communications and management. Often these positions were with international companies whose views of women in work were less traditional.

It is not unusual for women to have more than one job and to work part time in several places. This gives security in case one company closes down but it also makes it harder for women to compete for a career with men, who usually work full time for one company. There is a lot of legal protection for working mothers, but it is often hard for them to balance the demands of a career with looking after a family, especially as Argentinian families have traditionally been large.

9

The Way Ahead

In 1900, Argentina was described as one of the ten most prosperous countries in the world. The grand streets and impressive apartments of Recoleta and Palermo in Buenos Aires, which were built at that time, show this clearly enough. However, the twentieth century saw many changes that made Argentina poorer, not richer.

◄ An imposing view of central Buenos Aires: the 16-lane Avenida 9 de Julio, and the Obelisco, the monument built to commemorate the 400th anniversary of the founding of Buenos Aires.

Nevertheless, Argentina is still wealthier than some of its Latin American neighbours, such as Bolivia or Paraguay. The population is educated and resourceful. For many people, especially the middle classes of the cities, the economic recovery of the 1990s led to real advances in the quality of life. It reminded Argentinians of the national prosperity that could still be unlocked.

Argentina is once more at a crucial time. There are large groups – the majority of the population – living on the land, in the outlying provinces and in the *villas* who never really gained from the prosperity of the 1990s. These people are even poorer now than they were before Menem became president. Those who did benefit from the economic boom – the middle classes – feel disillusioned with the failure of politicians to guide the economy and nation through change.

The challenge now is to manage future change so that all groups in the country can share in the wealth of Argentina's resources. Then perhaps the hopes for the twentieth century will finally be realized in the twenty-first century.

▼ *The children of the* villas *need to share in Argentina's future development.*

IN THEIR OWN WORDS

'I am Dolores. This is my friend Nesle. We are finishing our last year at school and are about to start university here in Buenos Aires, where I will study Business and Management. Nesle will be studying Design and Fashion.

'We know our country has many difficulties at the moment but we believe that we have the potential and feeling of national solidarity to overcome our problems. The challenge is to work together to move forward and regain values of leadership that have been lost. We know this will take time and many changes may be needed but we are optimistic that this challenge can be met.'

Glossary

Agriculture Farming.

Basic literacy rate The percentage of the total adult population able to read and write.

Charcoal A fuel made by partially burning wood in a burner, without letting in any air.

Colonial Relating to a colony, a country that is ruled by another country. A colonial-style house in Argentina is one that looks like a Spanish house, because the Spanish used to rule Argentina.

Co-operative A business, such as a farm, that is owned by all the people who work for it and they all share the profits.

Credit Buying goods on credit means paying for them in small amounts over a period of time, after you have taken them home from the shop.

Delta An area of flat land where a river splits into several smaller channels just before it meets the sea.

Democracy A political system in which people choose the leaders they want to run the country by voting for them in elections.

Economic boom A time when businesses are doing well and plenty of jobs are available.

Economic depression A time when businesses struggle to produce and sell goods and many people are out of work.

Emissions Waste gases or liquids produced by industry or transport.

Exports Goods that are sold abroad.

Gaucho An Argentinian cowboy.

Glacier A large sheet of moving ice.

Global warming The increase in temperatures around the world, which many scientists believe is caused by an increase in pollution in the atmosphere.

GM seeds Genetically modified seeds, that is, seeds that have been changed in some way to make them produce a bigger crop, or resistant to disease.

GNP per capita GNP is Gross National Product, the amount of money that Argentina earns from all the goods and services it produces. 'Per capita' means 'per person', so GNP per capita is the total earned divided by the total population.

Hydroelectric power Electricity generated by turbines that are turned by the force of falling water.

Hyperinflation Very severe inflation, when prices rise extremely rapidly and people cannot afford to buy even basic goods such as food.

Immigrant Someone who has left his or her home country and come to live in another.

Imports Goods that are bought from other countries.

Indigenous Indigenous people are the first people to inhabit a country.

Infant mortality The number of deaths of children aged under one year; it is usually measured as the number of deaths per 1,000 children that are born.

International Monetary Fund An international organization set up after the Second World War to try to ensure worldwide economic stability. It lends money to governments that are in serious economic difficulty.

Latin America The countries of South and Central America that once belonged to Spain or Portugal and still have Spanish or Portuguese as their main language.

Life expectancy The average length of time that a person can expect to live.

Migrate To move from one area to another. Birds and animals migrate as the seasons change, in search of food. People might migrate in search of better jobs and living conditions.

Military coup The overthrow of a government by a group of military leaders who rely on the armed forces to enforce their laws, rather than gaining the support of the people in elections.

Plateau An area of high, fairly flat land.

Sanitation Services such as supplies of clean drinking water and sewers to take away waste water, which are needed to prevent the spread of disease.

Wholesaler Someone who buys goods in large quantities from manufacturers or farmers, for example, and sells them on in smaller quantities to shopkeepers.